This book belongs to:

....

ANIMAL SUPERPOWERS

How this collection works

This collection includes five amazing non-fiction texts that are ideal for encouraging your child's interest in animals, from those with incredible strength to the smallest creatures in the world! These texts are packed full of fascinating information, with the same high-quality artwork and photos you would expect from any non-fiction book – but they are specially written so that your child can read them for themselves. They are carefully levelled and in line with your child's phonics learning at school.

It's very important for your child to have access to non-fiction as well as stories while they are learning to read. This helps them develop a wider range of reading skills, and prepares them for learning through reading. Most children love finding out about the world as they read – and some children prefer non-fiction to story books, so it's doubly important to make sure that they have opportunities to read both.

How to use this book

Reading should be a shared and enjoyable experience for both you and your child. Pick a time when your child is not distracted by other things, and when they are happy to concentrate for about 15 minutes. Choose just one of the non-fiction texts for each session, so that they don't get too tired. Read the tips on the next page, as they offer ideas and suggestions for getting the most out of this collection.

Tips for reading non-fiction

STEP 1

Before your child begins reading one of the non-fiction texts, look together at the contents page for that particular text. What does your child think the text will be about? Do they know anything about this subject already? Briefly talk about your child's ideas, and remind them of anything they know about the topic if necessary. Look at the page of notes and 'before reading' suggestions for each text, and use these to help introduce the text to your child.

STEP 2

Ask your child to show you some of the non-fiction features in the text – for example, the contents page, glossary and index, photos, labels and fact boxes. Can your child tell you how the contents page and index help you to find your way around the text? Point out that some tricky words are explained in the glossary.

STEP 3

Ask your child to read the text aloud. Encourage them to stop and look at the pictures, and talk about what they are reading either during the reading session, or afterwards. Your child will be able to read most of the words in the text, but if they struggle with a word, remind them to say the sounds in the word from left to right and then blend the sounds together to read the whole word, e.g. *v-a-m-p-ire, vampire*. If they have real difficulty, tell them the word and move on.

STEP 4

When your child has finished reading, talk about what they have found out. Which bits of the text did they like most, and why? Encourage your child to do some of the fun activities that follow each text.

CONTENTS

Animal Superpowers.....................7

Super Senses.....................37

Minibeasts Matter! 59

Mini Marvels 81

Beaks and Feet.....................105

OXFORD
UNIVERSITY PRESS

Animal Superpowers

This text talks about some animals with amazing powers that help them survive where they live.

Before reading

Ask your child if they can think of any animals that can do amazing things that humans can't. For instance, spiders can spin silk to make strong webs.

Look out for ...

... a creature that can lick its own eyes

... a very strong ant

... an incredible long-jumping insect

... a fish that can swim five times faster than a human

... a bird that can see behind it without turning round

ANIMAL SUPERPOWERS

CONTENTS

Introduction.............................. 8

Super Strength! 10

Super Jumping! 12

Super Speed! 14

Super Distance! 16

Super Swinger! 18

Super Swimmer! 20

Super Sight! 22

Super Hearing! 24

Super Tongue! 26

Super Appetite! 28

Super Age! 30

Super Brain! 32

Glossary and Index 34

Isabel Thomas

Superheroes in films can do amazing things. But some animals have superpowers too!

Get ready to meet creatures that can:

run *fast*,

jump **high**

and carry **heavy** loads.

You will also meet animals that can:

hear using their feet,

see behind themselves

and lick their own eyeballs!

If you were as strong as an ant, you could carry 50 friends!

Leafcutter ants have strong necks and jaws. They can carry things 50 times heavier than themselves.

Weaver ants are super strong! They pull leaves together to build their nests.

Desert ants can pick up heavy food: dead insects!

How much can they lift?

human	leafcutter ant	rhinoceros beetle

1x own weight	50x own weight	100x own weight

Super Jumping!

If you jumped like a froghopper, you could leap over a skyscraper!

Froghoppers are tiny insects with a *big* talent.

Their back legs push against the ground very hard.
This pings the froghopper 70 centimetres into the air.

Froghoppers are less than a centimetre long. So this is like an adult human leaping 200 metres! It's a good way to escape **predators**.

Now you see me ...

... now you don't!

Super Speed!

If you ran like a tiger beetle, you could run 20 times faster than the best human runners!

Tiger beetles are the speediest insects. They can run about 120 times the length of their body *every second*.

How far in 1 second?

Tiger beetles use their super speed to hunt. They can catch almost any insect!

human: 6 body lengths

cheetah: 16 body lengths

tiger beetle: 120 body lengths

If you ran like an ostrich, you could finish a marathon in 50 minutes!

Ostriches run at up to 72 kilometres per hour. They run fast to escape from predators, such as lions.

The lions can run just as fast, but they get tired more quickly.

Ostriches' leg **joints** are very springy. This means they don't need to use much energy when they run.

How quickly could they run a **marathon**?

human	camel	ostrich

⏱ 2 hours plus	⏱ 1 hour	⏱ 50 minutes

Super Swinger!

If you moved like a gibbon, you could move 10 metres in just one swing!

Gibbons move by swinging from branch to branch. They can move as fast as a galloping horse!

curved fingers to
grab branches

Gibbons have wide
shoulders, long arms and
strong elbows.

legs shorter
than arms

light body

Gibbons can move around
and collect food from a large area.

19

If you swam like a sailfish, you could swim the length of a pool in 6 seconds!

Sailfish are the fastest fish. They can swim at up to 10 metres per second. This is five times faster than the best human swimmers.

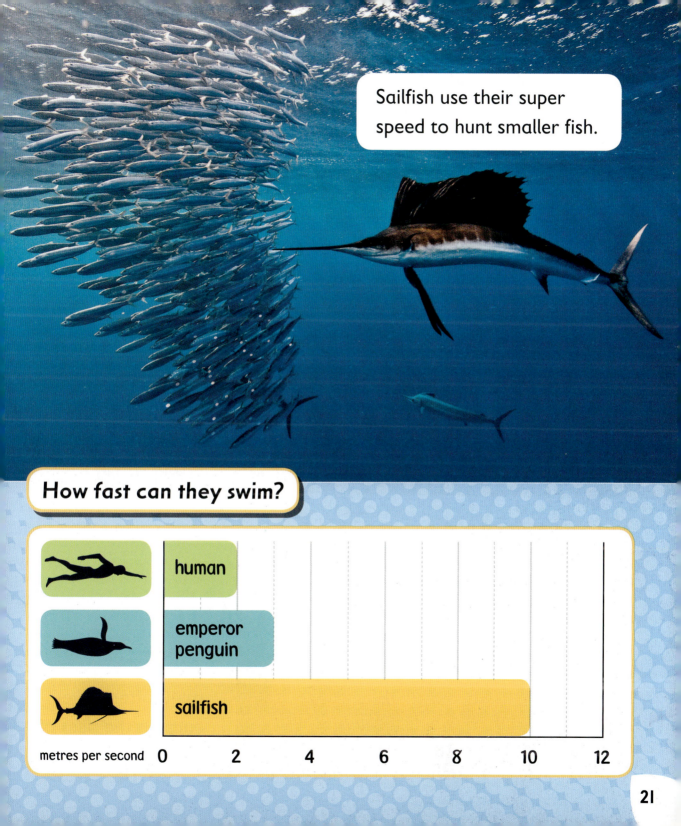

Sailfish use their super speed to hunt smaller fish.

How fast can they swim?

	metres per second
human	
emperor penguin	
sailfish	

metres per second 0   2   4   6   8   10   12

If you had eyes like a woodcock, you'd be able to see behind you!

Owls and other birds of prey have eyes that face forwards, like humans do.

But woodcocks and other birds that *are* **prey** often have eyes on the *sides* of their heads.

Woodcocks can see all around themselves without moving their heads.

Woodcocks can dig for food while looking out for predators, such as owls.

How far round can they see?

human	dog	woodcock

Super Hearing!

If you were a spider, you'd be able to hear with your feet!

Some spiders can hear sounds … but they don't have ears! These jumping spiders have tiny hairs on their legs, which can pick up sounds up to three metres away.

The spiders hide when they hear wasps buzzing. It can save them from getting caught.

Some wasps catch spiders and feed them to their babies.

hearing hairs on a spider's leg

Super Tongue!

If you were an okapi, you'd be able to lick your own eyeballs!

An okapi's (*say* oa-carp-ee) blue tongue can be up to 45 centimetres long. It comes in handy for cleaning their eyes, ears and even their nostrils!

How long is their tongue?

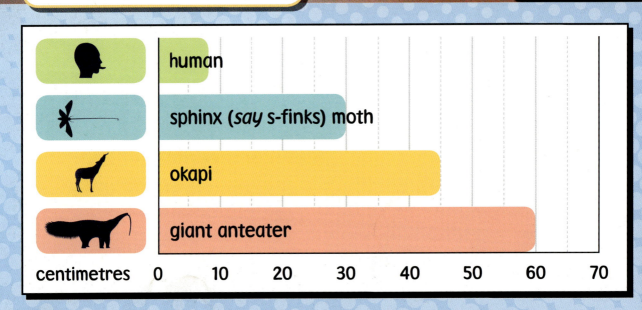

		human
		sphinx (*say* s-finks) moth
		okapi
		giant anteater

centimetres 0 10 20 30 40 50 60 70

Okapis' tongues are long and strong enough to pull leaves into their mouths.

Super Appetite!

If you had a caterpillar's appetite, you could eat 12 000 meals a day!

All caterpillars have big appetites. But these moth caterpillars are the greediest of all.

First, they eat their own egg case. Then they eat the leaf they hatched on. Then they start chomping other leaves. Each caterpillar eats 86 000 times its own weight in leaves before it changes into a moth!

The markings on the moth's wings look like eyes.

If you lived as long as a giant tortoise, you could have 250 birthday parties!

Wild giant tortoises live on islands far out at sea.

There are no predators to eat the giant tortoises on these islands. The tortoises live long, slow lives. They can live to be about 250 years old!

How many birthdays?

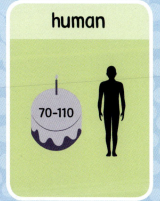

human

70-110

giant tortoise

250

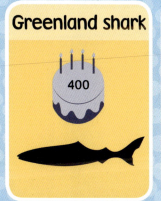

Greenland shark

400

ocean quahog*

500

* (*say* kwor-hog)

What's your superpower?

You can't outrun an ostrich or swim like a sailfish. A woodcock would spot you easily.

Even jumping spiders can hear you coming.

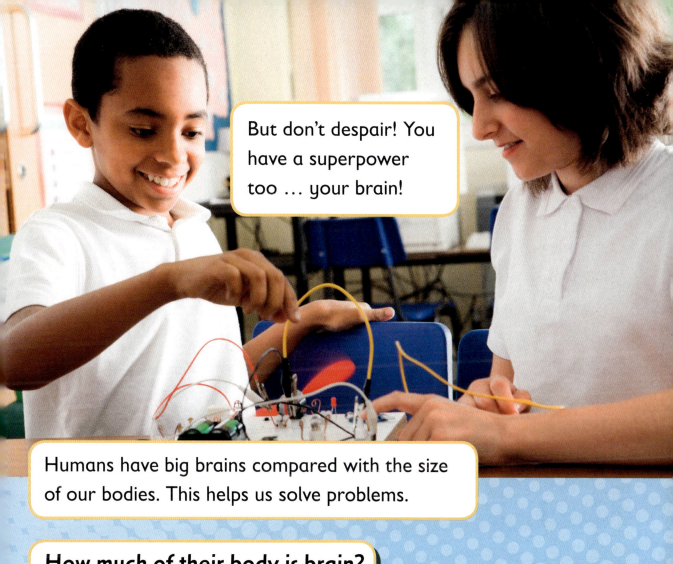

But don't despair! You have a superpower too … your brain!

Humans have big brains compared with the size of our bodies. This helps us solve problems.

How much of their body is brain?

horse	gorilla	bottlenose dolphin	human

Glossary

joints: where two bones fit together

marathon: long distance running race, usually 42.2 kilometres (26.2 miles) long

predators: animals that hunt other animals for food

prey: animals that are hunted by other animals as food

Index

ant	10–11	okapi	26–27
beetle	11, 14–15	ostrich	16–17, 32
froghopper	12–13	sailfish	20–21, 32
gibbon	18–19	spider	24–25, 32
human	11, 13, 15, 17, 20, 21, 22–23, 26, 31, 33	tortoise	30–31
		woodcock	22–23, 32
moth	26, 28–29		

Talk about it!

Which animal do you think has the most amazing superpower?

What is my superpower?

Match the animals with their superpowers.

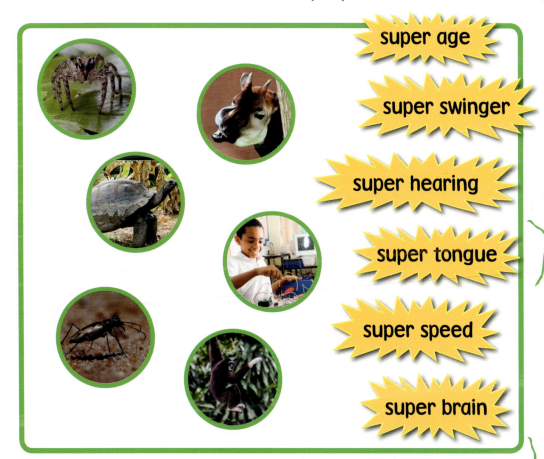

super age

super swinger

super hearing

super tongue

super speed

super brain

Super Senses

This text explores what the senses are and how they work, for both humans and animals. Read on and find out!

Before reading

Talk about our senses. Can your child name all five (sight, hearing, touch, taste, smell)?

Look out for ...

... a way of reading using dots

... a way of talking using your hands

... the reason you sometimes can't taste things when you have a cold

... an animal with eyes as big as its brain

... an insect that tastes things with its feet

SUPER SENSES

CONTENTS

Making Sense 38

Sending Messages 40

Seeing 42

Hearing 44

Tasting 46

Smelling 48

Touching 50

Animal Senses 52

Glossary and Index 56

Anita Ganeri

Making Sense

How do I find out what is going on around me?

I use my **senses**.

I see with my eyes.

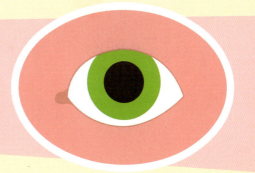

I hear with my ears.

I taste with my tongue.

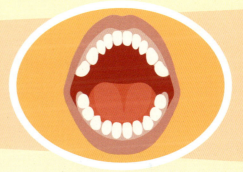

I smell with my nose.

I touch with my skin.

Sending Messages

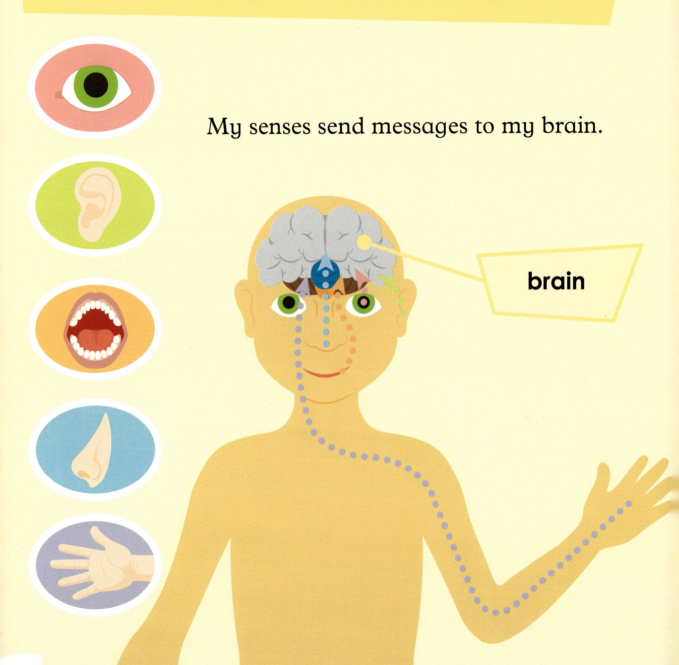

My senses send messages to my brain.

brain

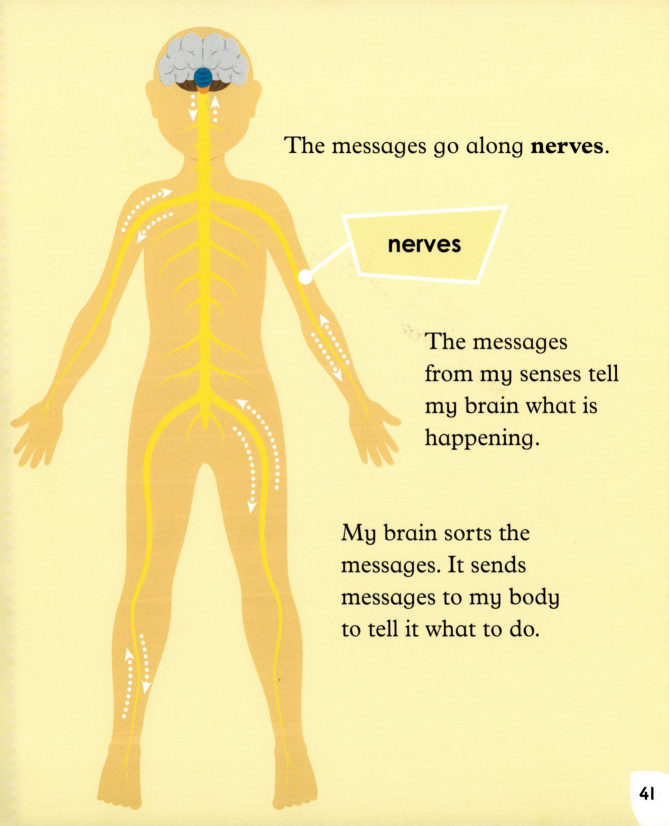

The messages go along **nerves**.

nerves

The messages from my senses tell my brain what is happening.

My brain sorts the messages. It sends messages to my body to tell it what to do.

Seeing

I see with my eyes. Light goes through tiny holes in the middle of my eyes. The light makes a picture. A message is sent to my brain. The picture is what I see.

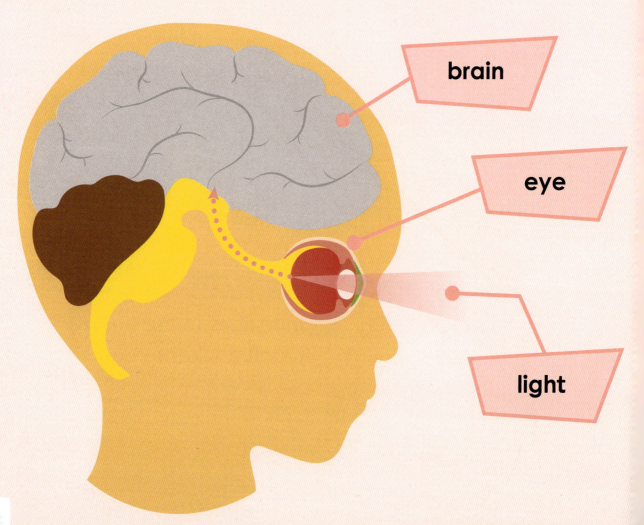

brain

eye

light

Some people wear glasses to help them see.

Glasses stop things looking fuzzy.

People who are blind find it difficult to see or cannot see.

This boy is using his sense of touch to read. He feels dots on the page.

Hearing

I hear with my ears.

Sounds go into my ear holes. Then they go along a tube into my ears.

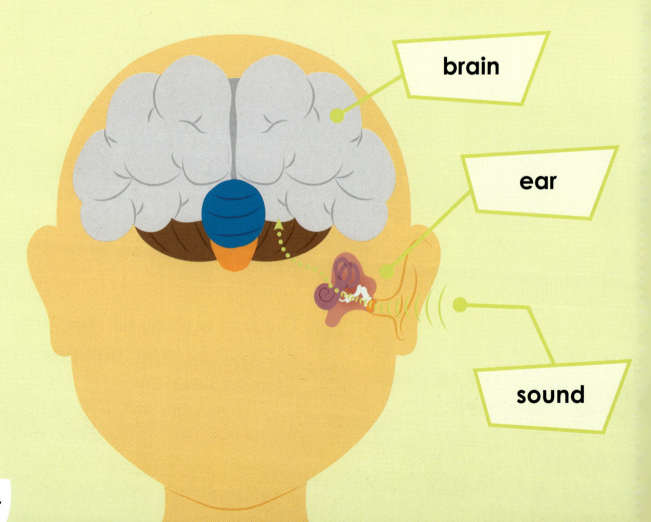

brain

ear

sound

Some people wear a hearing aid to help them hear.

A hearing aid makes sounds louder.

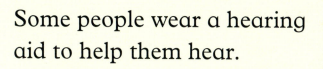

hearing aid

People who are deaf find it difficult to hear or cannot hear.

These children are talking using their hands.

Tasting

I taste with my tongue. My tongue has lots of tiny bumps, called **taste buds**.

tongue

taste buds

There are thousands of taste buds on my tongue.

When I eat, they pick up different tastes from my food.

sour taste

sweet taste

Smelling

I smell with my nose.

When I breathe in, smells from the air go up my nose.

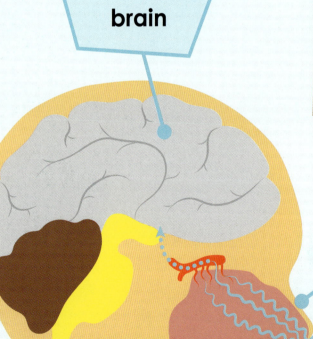

brain

nose

smell

My nose helps my tongue to taste my food.

If my nose is blocked, I cannot smell. This makes my food taste different.

Touching

I touch and feel things with my skin. My skin tells me if things are hot, cold, soft or hard.

The skin on my hands is good at feeling. When I stroke a cat, it feels soft and furry.

brain

touch

hand

A message is sent from the skin on my finger to my brain.

Animal Senses

Some animals have excellent senses.

Seeing

A **tarsier** has huge eyes for seeing in the dark.
Each eye is as big as its brain.

Hearing

Bats have very good hearing. Some can hear an insect walking on a leaf.

Tasting

A butterfly doesn't have a tongue. It tastes leaves with its feet. If the leaf tastes good, the butterfly lays eggs on it.

Smelling

Snakes use their tongues to smell. They flick their tongues in and out to get smells from the air.

Glossary

nerves: parts of your body that carry messages to and from your brain

senses: the main senses are sight, hearing, taste, smell and touch; you use your senses to find out what is going on around you

tarsier: a small furry animal that lives in trees in the rainforest

taste buds: tiny bumps on your tongue that you use to taste

Index

hearing   44–45, 53

nerves   41

seeing   42–43, 52

smelling   48–49, 55

tasting   46–47, 54

touching   50–51

Talk about it!

Which do you think was the most amazing fact in this text? Why?

Senses

Complete the crossword.

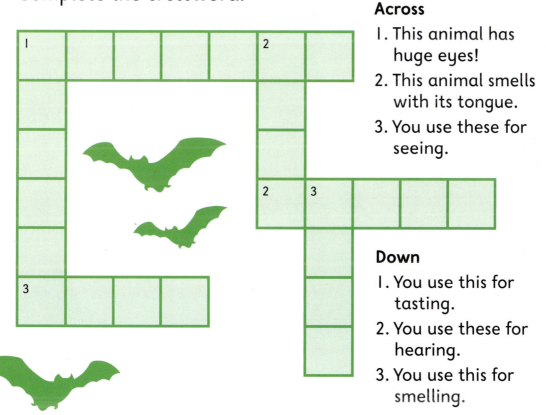

Across

1. This animal has huge eyes!
2. This animal smells with its tongue.
3. You use these for seeing.

Down

1. You use this for tasting.
2. You use these for hearing.
3. You use this for smelling.

Minibeasts Matter!

This text helps you find out about marvellous minibeasts, from bees to slugs – and discover why they matter!

Before reading

Talk about minibeasts. Has your child seen butterflies, insects, worms or other minibeasts? Which do they like best, and why?

Look out for ...

... a beetle that looks like it's made of gold

... a nest full of honey

... a minibeast that chomps on pests

... minibeasts that help clear up rubbish

... some minibeasts that people eat

MINIBEASTS MATTER!

CONTENTS

I Like Minibeasts 60

Minibeasts Look Fantastic! 62

This Minibeast Makes Honey 64

Minibeasts Make Better Soil 66

Minibeasts Get Rid of Pests 68

Minibeasts Spread Pollen 70

Minibeasts Clear Up Rubbish 72

Minibeasts Are Food 74

Minibeasts Matter! 76

Glossary and Index 78

Claire Llewellyn

I Like Minibeasts

I like minibeasts. These small animals are important and help us in many ways.

Did you know?
There are millions of different kinds of minibeast.

Some people don't like minibeasts.
I think they're wrong. Here are seven reasons
why minibeasts are the BEST!

Minibeasts Look Fantastic!

Let's look at some minibeasts close up.

This beetle looks like it's made of gold.

You can see through this dragonfly's wings.

This moth has beautiful wings with spots that look like eyes.

Did you know?

A dragonfly's eyes cover most of its head.

Every minibeast is different.

Aren't they fantastic?

This Minibeast Makes Honey

If you eat honey, you'll like this minibeast. It's the honeybee!

Honeybees visit flowers to suck up their nectar.

Honeybees collect the **nectar** and take it back to the nest. There they turn it into honey. They feed on the honey in the winter.

a bees' nest

Did you know?

Honeybees visit over two million flowers to make one jar of honey.

Minibeasts Make Better Soil

Many worms live under the ground. They burrow through the soil, and help to break it up. This makes it easier for plants to grow in the soil.

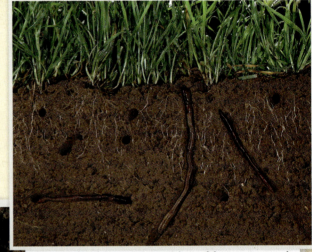

Worms burrow under the ground.

There may be more than two million worms in a field the size of a football pitch.

Minibeasts Get Rid of Pests

Pests spoil plants and crops. Farmers and gardeners like minibeasts that feed on pests.

Minibeasts eat all sorts of pests.

This spider catches pests in a web.

Did you know?
A hungry ladybird eats about 100 greenfly a day.

Minibeasts Spread Pollen

When a butterfly lands on a flower,
it picks up a yellow dust called **pollen**.

It spreads pollen from flower to flower.
The pollen helps the plants to make seeds.

Butterflies feed on flowers.

pollen

Did you know?

Bees, wasps and moths spread pollen too.

Minibeasts Clear Up Rubbish

What happens to food scraps, rotting plants and dead animals? Minibeasts help to clear them up. They make the world a cleaner place.

Some slugs and snails feed on rotting wood or fruit.

Did you know?

Slugs and snails have rows of tiny teeth to shred their food.

Minibeasts Are Food

Many animals feed on minibeasts. Fish, frogs, mice and birds feed on **insects**, worms and slugs.

Then bigger hunters, such as owls, sharks and bears eat the fish, frogs, mice and birds.

Did you know?
Many people around the world eat grasshoppers, **grubs** and snails.

Minibeasts Matter!

There are good reasons to like minibeasts.

They look amazing.

They make honey.

They make better soil.

They get rid of pests.

They spread pollen.

They clear up rubbish.

They are an important food.

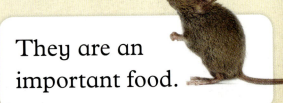

Glossary

grub: tiny creature that hatches from an insect's egg; it will become an insect

insect: animal with six legs, like a butterfly, bee or ant

nectar: sweet liquid inside a flower

pest: animal that spoils plants and crops

pollen: yellow dust inside flowers

Index

bee	64–65, 71
butterfly	70–71
flower	64–65, 70–71
pollen	70–71, 76
slug	72–73, 74
snail	72–73
spider	69
worm	66–67, 74

Talk about it!

How many flowers do honeybees visit to make one jar of honey?

Minibeast word search

Can you find all these minibeasts?

h	c	w	q	k	t	p	s	y	f
b	u	t	t	e	r	f	l	y	d
i	g	x	e	r	t	m	u	n	i
j	s	w	u	b	k	s	g	q	b
t	p	h	o	n	e	y	b	e	e
s	i	m	f	h	l	u	i	e	y
p	d	k	r	x	q	j	r	o	l
s	e	a	r	t	h	w	o	r	m
d	r	a	g	o	n	f	l	y	p

honeybee

earthworm

dragonfly

butterfly

slug

spider

79

Mini Marvels

This text explores some amazing tiny animals from around the world.

Before reading

Ask your child what is the smallest animal they can think of.
What is it like?

Look out for ...

... an extremely poisonous frog

... a bat that's almost as small as a bee

... a tiny, colourful bird that blends in with flowers

... a possum the size of a mouse

... a small but very dangerous octopus

MINI MARVELS

CONTENTS

Mini Marvels.................................... 82

A Micro Frog.................................. 84

A Seahorse So Small..................... 86

Pygmy Leaf Chameleon 88

Micro Bumblebee Bat.................. 90

Tiny Bee Hummingbird 92

Pygmy Possum 94

Blue-ringed Octopus 96

Flying Dragon 98

Mini Marvels Around the World 100

Glossary and Index...................... 102

Heather Hammonds

Mini Marvels

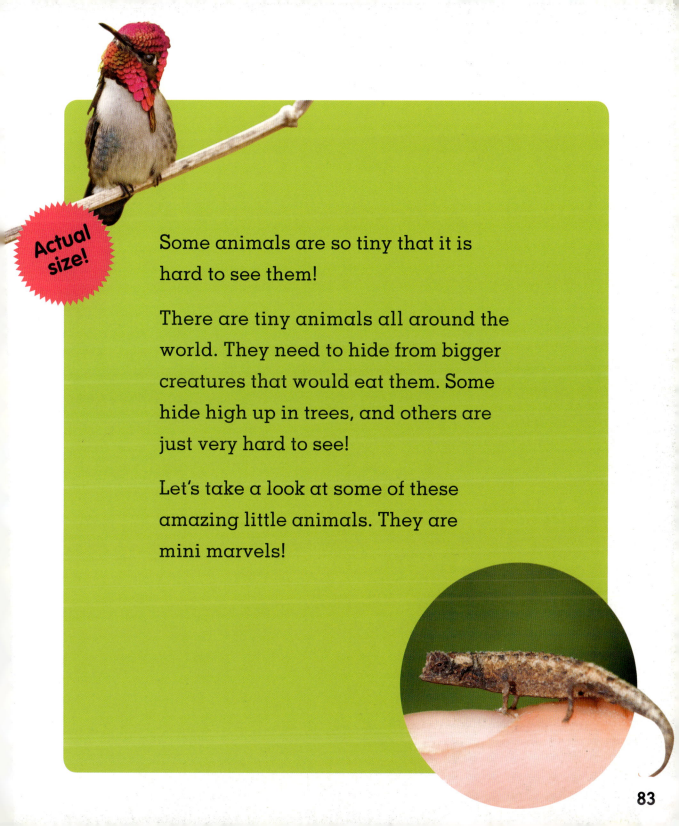

Actual size!

Some animals are so tiny that it is hard to see them!

There are tiny animals all around the world. They need to hide from bigger creatures that would eat them. Some hide high up in trees, and others are just very hard to see!

Let's take a look at some of these amazing little animals. They are mini marvels!

A Micro Frog

strawberry poison dart frog

Lives Rainforest, Central America

Eats Small bugs such as ants

Size About 2 centimetres (cm)

Actual size!

This little frog lives in the rainforest. Its bright colours warn other animals that it is very poisonous.

The tiny female frogs lay eggs. When tadpoles hatch from the eggs, they ride on their mother's back. She takes the tadpoles to live in a rainforest plant until they become frogs.

cm 1   2   3   4   5   6   7   8   9   10   11   12   13   14   15   16   17

A Seahorse So Small

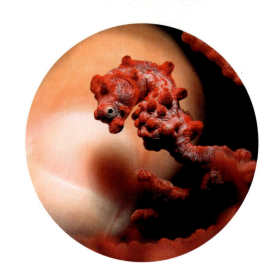

This amazing pygmy (say pig-me) seahorse is found on **coral reefs**. It looks like the coral, which helps it hide from **predators**.

The female seahorse lays eggs. Then the male seahorse looks after the eggs.

Around two weeks later, the eggs hatch. The baby seahorses swim away to find their own coral home.

Mini fact file

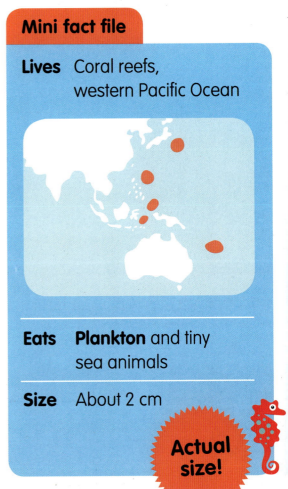

Lives	Coral reefs, western Pacific Ocean
Eats	**Plankton** and tiny sea animals
Size	About 2 cm

Actual size!

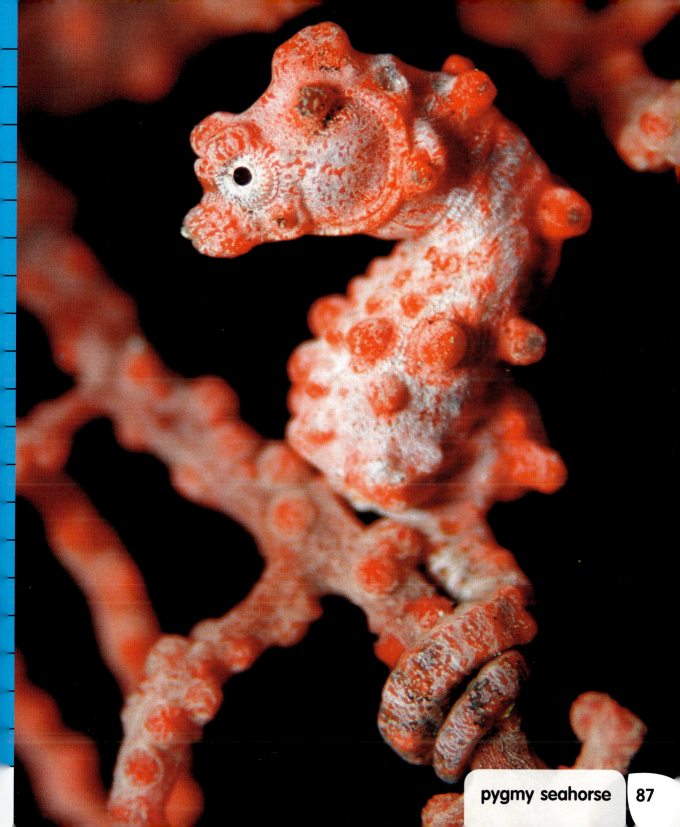

pygmy seahorse

Pygmy Leaf Chameleon

pygmy leaf chameleon

Mini fact file

Lives Forest, Madagascar

Eats Tiny insects

Size About 3 cm

Actual size!

This is one of the smallest chameleons (*say ka-meel-ee-ons*) in the world. It is so small when it's born, it can fit on your fingernail!

During the day, the chameleon hunts for insects on the ground. At night, it rests in small bushes. It uses its short tail to help it climb.

Like other kinds of chameleons, it can change colour to make it harder to see. This helps it hide from predators.

cm 1 2 3 4 5 6 7 8 9 10 11 12 13 14 15 16 17

Micro Bumblebee Bat

The bumblebee bat lives in dark caves. It sleeps during the day.

At sunset and sunrise, this bat zooms out of its cave to hunt insects.

It makes high squeaks. Then it listens for the sound to bounce back off juicy insects. That's how it finds its **prey**!

Mini fact file

Lives Myanmar and part of Thailand, South-East Asia

Eats Insects

Size About 3 cm

Actual size!

bumblebee bat

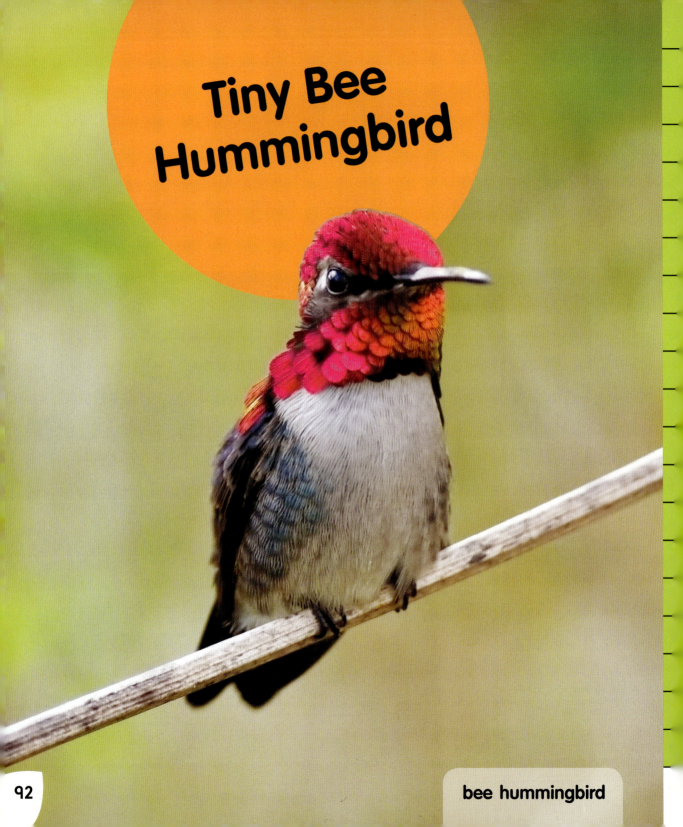

Tiny Bee Hummingbird

bee hummingbird

19
18
17
16
15
14
13
12
11
10
9
8
7
6
5
4
3
2
1
m

Mini fact file

Lives Island of Cuba, Caribbean

Eats Nectar from flowers

Size About 5.5 cm

Actual size!

The bee hummingbird is so tiny and fast that it's hard to see! It is the smallest bird in the world.

It zooms and zips from flower to flower. It eats the sweet **nectar** from flowers.

Its brightly coloured feathers help it blend in with the beautiful flowers.

Pygmy Possum

This possum is no bigger than a mouse! It goes out at night.

Using its strong claws and long tail, it hunts for food in the treetops.

The possum eats sweet nectar and pollen from forest flowers. Insects are on the menu, too.

Mini fact file

Lives Forest, Eastern Australia

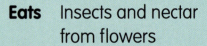

Eats Insects and nectar from flowers

Size About 9 cm, with a long thin tail

Actual size!

pygmy possum

cm 1   2   3   4   5   6   7   8   9   10   11   12   13   14   15   16   17

Blue-ringed Octopus

southern blue-ringed octopus

Mini fact file

Lives Oceans of southern Australia

Eats Shellfish such as crabs

Size About 15 cm

Actual size!

This octopus may be small, but it's one of the most poisonous creatures in the ocean! When it is upset, the blue rings on its body glow brightly. This warns animals to stay away.

This mini sea monster is a good hunter. It uses its poison to catch little crabs and other shellfish.

cm 1 2 3 4 5 6 7 8 9 10 11 12 13 14 15 16 17

Flying Dragon

flying dragon

cm 1

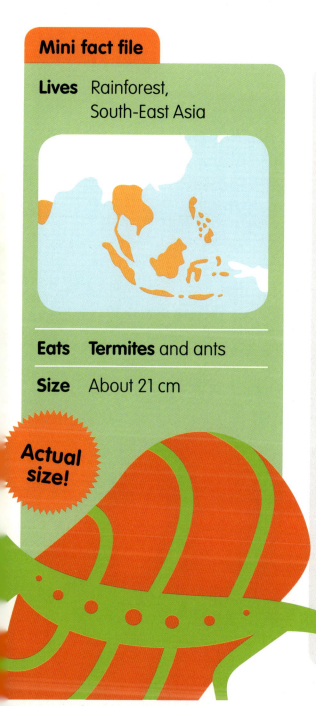
The flying dragon is a tiny lizard. It has very long ribs with skin between them. These look like wings.

The "wings" help it glide from tree to tree in the rainforest. It uses its long tail to steer.

It is not safe for this little lizard to spend much time on the ground. It would soon get eaten by predators. So it usually stays safely up in the tree branches, eating termites and ants.

4 5 6 7 8 9 10 11 12 13 14 15 16 17 18 19 20 21

Mini Marvels Around the World

Myanmar and part of Thailand, South-East Asia

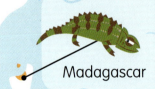

Madagascar

Oceans of southern Australia

Match each name to the correct animal.

strawberry poison dart frog   pygmy seahorse   pygmy leaf chameleon   bumblebee bat

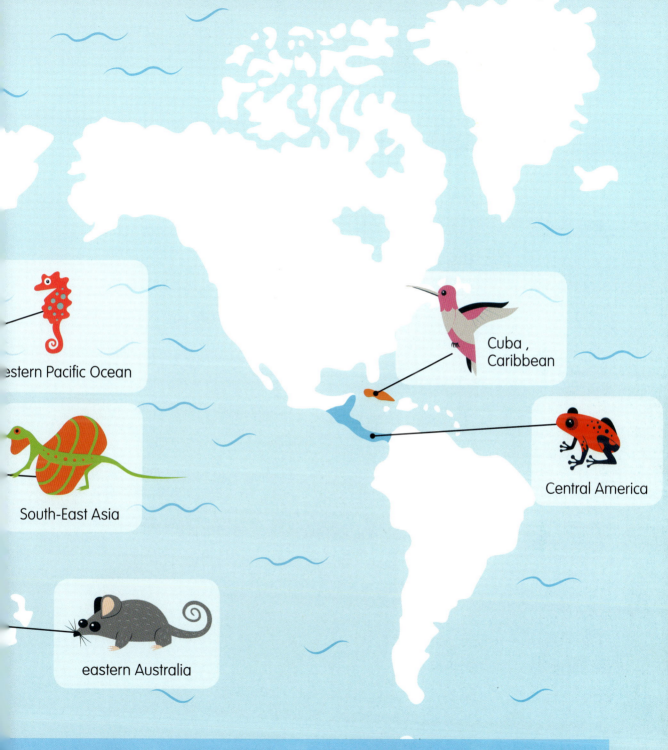

estern Pacific Ocean

Cuba , Caribbean

South-East Asia

Central America

eastern Australia

bee hummingbird   **pygmy possum**   **southern blue-ringed octopus**   **flying dragon**

Glossary

coral reefs: large groups of coral in the sea. Coral look like sea plants but are actually the hard skeletons of tiny sea animals called corals.

nectar: a sweet, sugary liquid found in the flowers of some plants

plankton: very tiny animals and plants that live in oceans and lakes

predators: animals that catch and eat other animals

prey: animals that are hunted and eaten by other animals

termites: small insects that eat wood

Index

bat	90-91
bird	92-93
chameleon	88-89
frog	84-85
lizard	98-99
octopus	96-97
possum	94-95
seahorse	86-87

Talk about it!

Which was your favourite tiny animal, and why?

Who is the smallest?

Number the animals from smallest to largest, starting with 1 for the smallest animal.

Beaks and Feet

This text uncovers some fascinating birds. Find out how their beaks and feet help them.

Before reading

Talk about birds with your child. Have they seen blackbirds, robins or other birds near where you live? What is their favourite type of bird?

Look out for ...

… a colourful, stripy beak

… a beak that can scoop up fish

… a bird that taps instead of singing

… chicks that gather together to stay safe

… a beak that doesn't belong to a bird!

BEAKS AND FEET

CONTENTS

Whose Stripy Beak Is This?.............. 106

Whose Hooked Beak Is This?........... 110

Whose Long Beak Is This?................ 114

Whose Pointed Beak Is This?........... 118

Whose Beak Is This?......................... 122

Glossary and Index.......................... 126

Mick Manning and Brita Granström

Whose Stripy Beak Is This?

This stripy beak belongs to an Atlantic puffin.

Atlantic puffins spend autumn and winter at sea. They only visit land in spring and summer to **breed**.

In the **breeding season**, puffins have bright beaks and orange feet. In autumn and winter, the colours of their beaks and feet fade.

Puffins have **webbed feet**. This helps them swim underwater and catch small fish. They can hold many fish in their large beaks.

To make a nest, puffins dig **burrows** in soft soil. The female lays an egg in the burrow. The egg hatches into a hungry chick called a puffling.

A puffling needs to be fluffy and fat to keep warm.

puffin

puffling

When pufflings are about six weeks old they leave the nest. They jump into the sea to join their parents … **PLOP!**

Whose Hooked Beak Is This?

This hooked beak belongs to an **osprey**.

Ospreys are large **birds of prey**
that eat fish. They hover above
the water, then dive in ...

SPLASH!

Ospreys have very sharp claws called
talons. They use their talons to catch
and hold the slippery, wriggly fish.

Some ospreys fly long distances to spend the winter in Africa. This is called **migration**.

This mother osprey has two chicks. She is feeding them tasty chunks of fish.

Whose **Long** Beak Is This?

This long beak belongs to an **Australian pelican**.

Pelicans mostly eat fish, but they also eat frogs and crabs. Some types of pelican dive underwater to catch their **prey**. Others scoop up food from the surface.

GULP!

The pouch of skin under a pelican's bill can stretch to scoop up water and fish. Then the water drains out, so the fish are trapped inside.

Pelicans have large webbed feet for paddling. Their feet are also good for walking in mud and sand.

This mother pelican is feeding her chicks.

Pelican chicks are born without feathers. As they get older, Australian pelican chicks gather together to stay safe from **predators**. The parents can recognise their own chicks at feeding time!

Whose Pointed Beak Is This?

This pointed beak belongs to a
green woodpecker.

Woodpeckers usually live in forests. They use their beaks to dig out beetle grubs from tree bark and rotten wood. They also eat fruit, nuts and **sap**.

Woodpeckers peck out tunnels to make their nests in tree trunks. The females lay around four eggs in the nest.

TAP!

TAP!

TAP!

Woodpeckers can't sing. Instead, they tap very fast on trees, poles or even chimneys. This is called drumming.

great spotted
woodpecker

There are lots of
different types of
woodpecker.

black
woodpecker

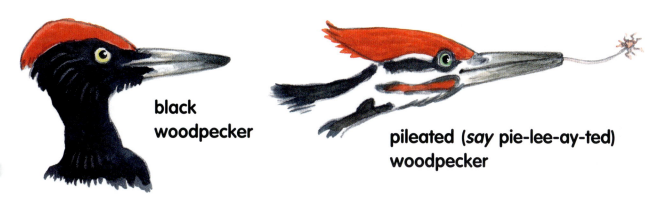

pileated (*say* pie-lee-ay-ted)
woodpecker

Woodpeckers have long, sticky tongues. Their
tongues reach inside holes to get at beetle
grubs and ants' eggs.

tree
trunk

Most woodpeckers have four toes – two pointing
forwards and two pointing backwards. Their toes
are good for gripping onto tree trunks.

Whose Beak Is This?

Is it a duck?
Is it a goose?

This is not a bird's beak. It belongs to a **platypus!**

A platypus is a very unusual **mammal**. It has fur and it feeds its babies on milk, like other mammals. But it also has a beak and lays eggs!

Platypuses use their beaks to find food in the water. They like to eat insects, tadpoles, shrimps and crayfish. They dive and swim underwater using their webbed feet.

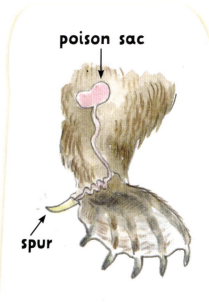

poison sac

spur

A platypus looks very cute and cuddly — but watch out! The male has **spurs** on his back legs that can sting.

The male's spur is poisonous.

OUCH!

Glossary

birds of prey: birds, such as hawks and eagles, that catch and eat other animals.

breed: to have babies

breeding season: the time when an animal has its babies, often in the spring

burrows: tunnels or holes that animals dig and live in

mammal: an animal that usually gives birth to live baby animals and feeds them milk

migration: when birds move to a different/warmer climate for part of the year

predators: animals that hunt and eat other animals

prey: animals that are hunted and eaten by other animals

sap: something thick and sticky that can be found in trees and plants

spurs: sharp spikes on a foot or leg

webbed feet: feet with toes that are joined together with pieces of skin

Index

breeding	108	poison	125
mammal	124	predators	117
migration	113	puffin	108–109
osprey	112–113	webbed feet	109, 117, 124
pelican	116–117	woodpecker	120–121
platypus	124–125		

Talk about it!

I'm going to be a puffin when I grow up. Can you remember what I'm called?

Name that beak!

Match the beaks with their owners.

pelican

platypus

puffin

osprey

OXFORD
UNIVERSITY PRESS

Great Clarendon Street, Oxford, OX2 6DP, United Kingdom

Oxford University Press is a department of the University of Oxford. It furthers the University's objective of excellence in research, scholarship, and education by publishing worldwide. Oxford is a registered trade mark of Oxford University Press in the UK and in certain other countries

Animal Superpowers text © Isabel Thomas 2018
Illustrations © Tim Bradford 2018

Super Senses text © Oxford University Press 2018
Illustrations © Sara Lynn Cramb 2018

Minibeasts Matter! text © Oxford University Press 2018
Illustrations © Nanette Regan 2018

Mini Marvels text © Heather Hammonds 2014
Illustrations © Tim Bradford 2014

Beaks and Feet text © Mick Manning and Brita Granstrom 2014
Illustrations © Mick Manning 2014

The moral rights of the authors have been asserted

This Edition published in 2020

British Library Cataloguing in Publication Data
Data available

ISBN: 978-0-19-277386-9

10 9 8 7 6 5 4 3 2 1

Paper used in the production of this book is a natural, recyclable product made from wood grown in sustainable forests. The manufacturing process conforms to the environmental regulations of the country of origin.

Printed in China

Acknowledgements
Series Editor: Nikki Gamble

Animal Superpowers

The publisher would like to thank the following for permission to reproduce photographs: **p8:** blickwinkel/Alamy Stock Photo; **p9:** Joseph Quinn/123RF; p10: Redmond Durrell/Alamy Stock Photo; **p10:** FLPA/Alamy Stock Photo; **p11:** Premaphotos/Alamy Stock Photo; **p12:** HEATH MCDONALD/Science Photo Library; **p13:** Stephen Dalton/Minden Pictures/Getty; **p13:** Bert Pijs/NiS/Minden Pictures/Getty; **p14:** Auscape/Getty; **p15:** Tina Jeans/Shutterstock; **p16&32:** LOOK Die Bildagentur der Fotografen GmbH/Alamy Stock Photo; **p17:** Mint Images - Frans Lanting/Getty; **p18:** Manoj Shah/Getty; **p19:** Arco Images Gmbh/Alamy Stock Photo; **p20&32:** Doug Perrine/Getty; **p21:** Image Source/Alamy Stock Photo; **p22:** Jeffrey P Miller/Shutterstock; **p22&32:** Nature Picture Library/Alamy Stock Photo; **p23:** Nature Bird Photography/Shutterstock; **p24:** Thomas Marent/Minden Pictures/Getty; **p24&32:** Chua Wee Boo/Getty; **p25:** Hotforphotog/Shutterstock; **p26:** Andra Boda/EyeEm/Getty; **p27:** blickwinkel/Alamy Stock Photo; **p28:** Russell Burden/Getty; **p29:** Stone Nature Photography/Alamy Stock Photo; **p30:** heinzelmannfrank/iStock; **p31:** Tui De Roy/Minden Pictures/FLPA

Super Senses

The publisher would like to thank the following for permission to reproduce photographs: **p43t:** dolgachov/iStockphoto; **p43b:** wavebreakmedia/Shutterstock; **p45t:** kavring / Alamy Stock Photo; **p45b:** Brian Mitchell/Getty Images; **p47t:** sarahwolfephotography/Getty Images; **p47b:** evgenyatamanenko/123RF; p48: SIP SA/Alamy Stock Photo; **p51:** Liz Banfield/Getty Images; **p52:** Ondrej Prosicky/Shutterstock; **p53:** Gunter Ziesler/Getty Images; **p54:** Muhammad Naaim/Shutterstock; **p55:** Donald M. Jones/Minden Pictures/Getty Images.

Minibeasts Matter!

The publisher would like to thank the following for permission to reproduce photographs: **p61:** Nailia Schwarz/123RF; **p61:** GlobalP/iStockphoto; **p61:** Aconia/iStockphoto; **p62tl:** BLANCHOT Philippe/hemis.fr/Getty Images; **p62:** David Chapman/Alamy Stock Photo; **p62bl:** Matt Dobson/Dreamstime; **p63:** BIOSPHOTO/Alamy Stock Photo; **p63tl:** Thomas Marent/Minden Pictures/Getty Images; **p63tl:** dmbaker/iStockphoto; **p64:** Nature Photographers Ltd/Alamy Stock Photo; **p64t:** MichaelGMeyer/iStockphoto; **p64-65:** iSidhe/iStockphoto; **p65b:** Brian Stablyk/Getty Images; **p66b:** Nigel Cattlin / Alamy Stock Photo; **p66t:** Auscape International Pty Ltd/Alamy Stock Photo; **p67:** ap-images/iStockphoto; **p68b:** lensblur/iStockphoto; **p69l:** wendydrent/iStockphoto; **p68l:** Brian Bevan/Alamy Stock Photo; **p68r:** Nigel Cattlin/Alamy Stock Photo; **p71b:** SumikoPhoto/iStockphoto; **p70:** Vojtaheroutcom/Megapixl.com; **p71:** Cute Kitten Images/Getty Images; **p69r:** Nic Hamilton/Alamy Stock Photo; **p71t:** Tinus Tibbe/Alamy Stock Photo; **p73r:** SergeyToronto/iStockphoto; **p72t:** Hayashi/EyeEm/Getty Images; **p73l:** MaRoPictures/iStockphoto; **p75b:** shakzu/iStockphoto; **p74tl:** Dave Watts/Alamy Stock Photo; **p74bl:** F1 Online/REX/Shutterstock; **p74tr:** Nature Photographers Ltd/Alamy Stock Photo; **p75t:** Thomas Hanahoe/Alamy Stock Photo; **p74br:** J.-L. Klein and M.-L. Hubert/FLPA.

All other photographs by Shutterstock

Mini Marvels

The publisher would like to thank the following for permission to reproduce photographs: **p82:** Ern Mainka/Alamy; **p82/83:** Kevin Elsby/Alamy; **p83:** Barrie Britton/Nature Picture Library; **p84:** John Cancalosi/Nature Photo Library; **p85:** Mlorenzphotography/Getty Images; **p86:** Reinhard Dirscherl/Getty Images; **p87:** Reinhard Dirscherl/Getty Images; **p88:** Panoramic Images/Getty Images; **p89:** Panoramic Images/Getty Images; **p90:** Merlin D Tutle/Getty Images; **p91:** Steve Downer/ardea.com; **p92:** Kevin Elsby/Alamy; **p93:** Kevin Elsby/Alamy; **p95:** Gary Lewis/Getty Images; **p94:** NHPA/photoshot; **p96:** Gary Bell/OceanwideImages.com; **p97:** Gary Bell/OceanwideImages.com; **p98:** Jean Paul Ferrero/ardea.com; **p99:** Premaphotos/Alamy; **p102:** Mlorenzphotography/Getty Images

All other images Shutterstock

Cover images Shutterstock